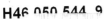

1950s BRITAIN

17/Mar/2011

How we worked · How we played · How we lived

First published in Great Britain in 2010 by Shire
Publications Ltd, Midland House, West Way, Botley,
Oxford OX2 0PH, United Kingdom.
44-02 23rd Street, Suite 219, Long Island City, NY11101,
USA.

E-mail: shire@shirebooks.co.uk www.shirebooks.co.uk

© 2010 Shire Publications

Every attempt has been made by the Publishers to secure
the appropriate permissions for materials reproduced in
this book. If there has been any oversight we will be happy
to rectify the situation and a written submission should be
made to the Publishers.

A CIP catalogue record for this book is available from the
British Library.

Shire Living Histories no. 2 • ISBN-13: 978 0 74780 779 7

Robert Pearce has asserted his right under the Copyright,
Designs and Patents Act, 1988, to be identified as the
author of this book.

Designed by Myriam Bell Design, France and typeset in
Perpetua, Jenson Text and Gill Sans.
Printed in China through Worldprint Ltd.

10 11 12 13 14   10 9 8 7 6 5 4 3 2 1

ACKNOWLEDGEMENTS

Illustrations are acknowledged as follows:

Corbis, pages 28 and 41; Getty Images, pages 4, 8,
9 (top and bottom), 10 (bottom), 12, 14 (top and
bottom), 15, 25, 26 (bottom), 30, 32, 35 (top and
bottom), 36, 43 (bottom), 44, 52 (top), 55 (bottom), 57,
60 (bottom), 62 (bottom), 66, 68, 69 (top), 70, 71, 72,
74, 75 (bottom), 76 (top and bottom), and 77; Mary Evans
Picture Library, pages 6, 24 (top and bottom), 29, and 33;
Mirrorpix, pages 11, 18, 26 (top), and 75 (top); The
Robert Opie Collection, pages 10 (top), 16, 17, 19, 23,
27, 34, 38, 40 (left and right), 42, 43 (top), 44, 47
(top and bottom), 48 (top and bottom), 49, 50, 52
(bottom), 54, 55 (top), 56, 58, 60 (top), 61, 62 (top),
63 (top), 63 (bottom), 64, 69 (bottom); Science and
Society Picture Library, page 53; Shire Books/Nick
Hardcastle, pages 20–1.

Shire Publications is supporting the Woodland Trust, the UK's leading woodland conservation charity, by funding the dedication of trees.

CONTENTS

PREFACE

THE 1930s have been called a 'dark valley' between the twin precipices of depression and war, a time of hardship and grind relieved only by glimpses of the escapist Hollywood glamour on offer at the picture-palaces that sprang up on every high street. There is no doubt that, for many, this picture – the England of George Orwell – is true, but of course, it is only one part of the story, and no summary can ignore the modernism that was expressed in many ways, the rise of electrical consumer goods, suburban ribbon development (the world gently satirised by John Betjamin) and the social advances such as paid holidays. The contrasts were well documented at the time, and have been picked up on by many historians ever since.

Nevertheless, a life of hard work, few physical comforts and ever-present fear of unemployment was the grim reality for many Britons, particularly those living in the industrial and mining towns of the north, and in this volume Robert Pearce – drawing on memoirs of the men and women who lived there – takes us to the mills, into the terraces and down the streets of Blackburn, Lancashire, to meet the people who knew little but this pinched existence. He stresses, though, that while life in Blackburn may have been typical in many ways, it was not the only type of life available to Britons. Indeed, contemporary commentators such as J. B. Priestley talked of 'three Englands', quite distinct culturally, economically and geographically, and Professor Pearce also looks at this land of contrasts and introduces the varied people who, despite all their difficulties, were shortly to face, and overcome, the greatest challenge in their national history.

Peter Furtado
General Editor

Opposite:
Holidaymakers
on the beach at
Blackpool in
1939. The woman
in the foreground
seems dressed
rather for
a funeral, but
a variety of
fashions is in
fact visible.

INTRODUCTION

BLACKBURN, LANCASHIRE, was no stranger to unemployment, and it was not at all unusual to see a queue outside the Labour Exchange. Yet no one could remember seeing quite so many drably dressed men lined up – and they were men, with no women and very few youths – as in the final months of 1932. Not only was the queue long, it was slow-moving, and there was plenty of time for conversations, some being private talks between individuals, some heated discussions in which several would partake.

Many complained about the benefits system. Benefits had been cut by 10 per cent the previous year, and the clerks seemed to delight in treating the unemployed harshly. 'They treat you like a lump of dirt, they do.' Also, the new means test took into account the income of the whole household, so that if a son worked part-time as an errand boy his father would not receive the full rate of benefit. A small group of men were worried that their dole would be docked because they had recently returned from a protest march to London. At each town the contingent of hunger marchers had been fed by local volunteers – generally with bread, mashed potatoes and tea – and at each stop their numbers had grown. By the time they reached London their petition contained a million signatures, but it had been seized by the police and the men had not been allowed into Downing Street. Now these men let it be known exactly what they thought of the government, and some who had fought in the Great War were especially bitter, recalling phrases about a 'land fit for heroes'.

Other men debated the causes of the mass unemployment that was afflicting Britain. Some recalled previous slumps in the local cotton industry and said that the good times would return, sooner or later, as they always had before. Things would 'allus' get better. 'Come on, lads, it'll be aw reet!' Others were more pessimistic, insisting that this slump was different. Hadn't there been a crash on the stock market in Wall Street in 1929, and wasn't unemployment high – and

Opposite:
The National
Grid, begun
in 1928 and
completed
in 1934,
revolutionised
life for many in
the 1930s. This
illustration shows
the sub-station
at Yoker, near
Glasgow, with
a tower carrying
transmission lines
across the Clyde.

Pawnbrokers flourished in areas affected by unemployment or low pay in the 1930s. Neighbourhood youths would often use the three gilt balls as target practice.

Opposite bottom: The most famous of all the hunger marches, the Jarrow Crusade of 1936, led by a harmonica band. The men were allowed to present a petition to Parliament, but no help was forthcoming.

getting worse — in countries like the United States and Germany? One or two men even said that the capitalist system was breaking down and that maybe Stalin and the Communists in Russia had the right idea. A few decided that emigration might be the answer. Newspapers revealed that there were two million more people in Britain than a decade before, so that there were almost forty million in England and Wales alone. Perhaps there was a better life to be had in Canada, Australia or New Zealand. Others thought the answer was closer to home, in the Midlands or the south, and most knew of younger men, without families, who had gone to try their luck in Birmingham, London or elsewhere.

Other men had more private worries. One was uncertain how he'd ever get his best suit of clothes out of hock at the local pawnshop. Another was keen to get back to his allotment, though a third did not mind the queuing, even in this cold weather, as it was at least a rest from the incessant tramping of the streets in search of work that seemed to fill his days. Several men were unhappy that their wives or daughters had had to take jobs as servants in some of the big houses on the outskirts of the town. The health of their children was a cause for concern, while one man was proud to have got his fifteen-year-old son into the army. The boy had not wanted to enlist, but he had no choice. Now at least he would be well fed, and there was surely no chance of another war, not after the 'war to end war' in 1914–18.

Others chatted about sport, the poultry they kept, the new radio they had heard, and a hundred and one other things. Some were taciturn, just looking around. One man even counted the number of factory chimneys to be seen, far more than in previous years when these chimneys had been belching out smoke and the air was thick and visibility poor. Some waited without thought, with a vague awareness of hunger or anxiety about the future gnawing at their stomachs.

This snapshot of a town in the northwest of England was in some ways typical of Britain in the 1930s, a decade marked in the popular imagination by the dole queue, the hunger march, unemployment and poverty. The industrial areas of Britain — which had produced the coal, iron and steel, ships and textiles that had made the country wealthy in the previous century – were massively depressed in the early 1930s. In Lancashire, employment in the mining and textile industries declined, while in some other parts of the country the situation was even worse. In MerthyrTydfil in south Wales, for instance, the closure of coalmines meant that around 60 per cent of workers were on the dole, and in Jarrow ('the town that was murdered'), in the northeast of England, more like three-quarters were thrown on the dole when Palmers' shipbuilding yard was closed. Nor was it much better on the Clyde in Glasgow, or in Belfast, where shipbuilders Harland andWolff had to lay off workers.

The chimneys of cotton mills belch out their smoke over Manchester, the original 'Cottonopolis', in the early 1930s. The houses in the foreground are typical workers' cottages.

There was indeed a gloomy side to the 1930s, though British people still contrived to live their lives with dignity and courage. They did not go to pieces; instead they simply made the best of things. There could even be, in the title of Walter Greenwood's classic novel about the slump of the early 1930s in Lancashire, *Love on the Dole*.

The radio, or wireless set, became a must-buy for those whose homes were wired for electricity in the 1930s. The old heavy industries might be declining, but new consumer goods industries were flourishing.

In addition, there was soon economic improvement. Unemployment peaked in Britain in December 1932, and thereafter there was a recovery. The worldwide depression lifted as the effects of the stock-market crash were overcome. This did not solve the problems of over-production in Britain's 'staple industries', whose goods were simply not needed in such large quantities any longer, and the famous Jarrow hunger march took place as late as 1936; but the dole queues in Blackburn and many other places fell. Things seemed to be getting back to normal, though normality in Lancashire meant more than 10 per cent on the dole.

Yet in some parts of the country there was significant economic expansion. Most of those who 'got on their bikes' in search of work further south did indeed find it, and nationally Britain did not merely recover from the Depression, it began to boom. With the expansion of the electricity industry, and the construction of the National Grid, many employment opportunities arose in new consumer goods industries, producing radios, vacuum cleaners and other devices. Furthermore, car production grew and house-building flourished. The era of the dole queue and poverty was also the era of new labour-saving devices, of conspicuous consumption and of a new materialism.

Britain was a highly varied country in the 1930s. The novelist J. B. Priestley certainly found this when he travelled the length of England in the autumn of 1933, starting in Southampton and journeying via Bristol and the Cotswolds to the Midlands, the northwest of England, Yorkshire and the northeast, and then home via Lincolnshire and East Anglia. He concluded that he had not just seen England, he had 'seen a lot of Englands'. He could discern at least three. There was the pre-industrial England

Local boys look on with obvious amusement at the garb of Harrow schoolboys in 1937. The decade was the best of times for some, the worst of times for others, and there was little class mobility.

of the southernmost counties, 'Old England, the country of the cathedrals and manor houses and inns, of Parson and Squire'. Then there was 'the nineteenth-century England, the industrial England of coal, iron, steel, cotton, wool, railways; of thousands of rows of little houses all alike'. There was also the new England, marked by light industries,

the England of arterial and by-pass roads, of filling stations and factories that look like exhibition buildings, of giant cinemas and dance halls and cafes ... It is a large-scale, mass-production job, with cut prices. You could almost accept Woolworths as its symbol.

The cinema is as much a symbol of the 1930s as the dole queue. The largest cinemas – often called Odeon, Astoria or Gaumont – could seat up to 2,000 people. The Odeon shown here was at Kingston upon Thames, photographed in 1935.

But there were other Englands besides these, for instance the England of the very rich and that of the poverty-stricken, the unemployed often being set aside, living in certain districts where in almost every house in street after street the householder had no work. In addition, of course, the United Kingdom was made up not only of England, however many Englands there were, but of Wales, Scotland and Northern Ireland.

Furthermore, Priestley was only writing about a certain time. There is a sharp contrast between Britain in the throes of depression in 1932 and Britain in 1937, when national production was almost 50 per cent higher. By this latter date, many people had more leisure, smaller families and more disposable income, and they were living longer and doing so in better houses. Social life was changing. Local cultures still existed and in many ways flourished, for Britain was indeed a very varied place. Yet new social trends were felt everywhere, and certainly Lancashire towns like Blackburn were not immune. New mass-produced goods were aimed, by definition, at a mass market, and they were to be seen everywhere, as were advertisements for them. Similarly, all were affected by mass communications: almost everyone listened to the radio and went to the cinema, and many read the same magazines and books. Critics complained of a new uniformity in Britain. Certainly all were affected by Britain's declaration of war against Nazi Germany on 3 September 1939. There was no rejoicing, as there had been back in 1914, just a gritty national acceptance of the new trials to come.

FAMILY LIFE

THE SCIENCE OF STATISTICS took a giant leap forward in the 1930s. Facts were collected, collated and analysed on almost every conceivable topic. The end result was that people were told what they could already see for themselves, for instance that the size of the nuclear family was declining. By the end of the 1930s the average British married couple had two children, or 2.2 to be precise. But of course averages could disguise a multitude of variations, and working-class families tended to be larger. There was nothing surer, according to the lyrics of a popular song of the time: 'The rich get rich and the poor get children'.

Yet even poorer families were becoming smaller, and this was certainly not due to any rise in the numbers of deaths. Infant mortality fell significantly in the 1930s, though of course most sharply in affluent areas. Instead it was due to various forms of birth control. By 1935 the London Rubber Company was making about two million condoms ('male appliances') every year. But each packet cost at least a shilling, and more common methods of preventing conception included the 'safe period' (though the 'experts' disagreed on when exactly in the monthly cycle this occurred), male withdrawal or simply abstention. Abortions were illegal, unless it was to save the life of the mother, but there were a number of methods of inducing a miscarriage – from herbal remedies to violent exercise, scalding hot baths and copious draughts of gin. A government committee estimated in 1939 that as many as 66,000 foetuses had been in some way aborted in Britain since 1918.

There is no doubt that, whatever its size, the family was a strong and resilient institution in Britain in the 1930s. Proven adultery was the only grounds for divorce until 1937, when the law was changed to add desertion for three years, cruelty, rape, sodomy, bestiality, habitual drunkenness, incurable insanity, venereal disease and non-consummation to the list of divorcable offences. The number of divorces doubled between 1930 and 1940, but even so

Opposite:
A woman's work was never done in the 1930s. Here a housewife in 1939 takes on cleaning work outside the home to supplement the family income.

Having no garden, it was customary for housewives to string a washing line across the street. She would then use a prop to raise the line to enable the waiting car to pass.

Working-class families tended to be close in the 1930s – literally so with this family having their tea together in 1938. Yet the average size of families had begun to fall.

at the latter date only 8,396 couples untied the knot. Very few of these lived in working-class towns like Blackburn. Here divorce was no more on the agenda than 'living in sin' or overt homosexuality. Marriage existed till death parted the couple, and

family units tended to be close-knit, with parents and grandparents often living close together.

It was the family unit which helped the unemployed survive the depression of the 1930s. This was certainly the verdict of George Orwell, who spent the early months of 1936 in Lancashire. He had seen much more destitution in London, where homeless people would often walk the streets by day before spending the night in a cheap doss-house, if they could afford it. There were no beggars in Wigan and precious few in Manchester or Liverpool. 'Life is still fairly normal ... Families are impoverished, but the family-system has not broken up.'

Family traditions were being maintained at a time when, politically, women had equal rights with men. Beginning in 1929, women had the vote on exactly the same terms as men, so that everyone aged twenty-one or over could vote. In fact, there were more female than male voters. Even so, in a northern working-class home, there were sharply defined gender roles. The mother would be in charge of the house, which basically meant extremely hard work. One day a week would be wash day. Clothes would bubble in

A group of boys in the 1930s gain enormous pleasure from a game of cricket in the street. The huge bat is obviously home-made, while the wicket is an upturned suitcase.

An advertisement from 1935 for a new vacuum cleaner. If a woman was to 'keep young and beautiful' she needed an array of labour-saving devices, of which this was one of the most important.

the copper for as long as was needed to get them spotless, so that the kitchen would be full of steam for most of the day. If it was wet outside, so that it was no use stringing a washing line across the street, items would be left to dry indoors. Also once a week a woman would clean her doorstep and window-sills, and often the portion of the pavement outside the front door, with a 'rubbing stone' – and woe betide anyone who walked across it with muddy boots! There were also everyday chores, like ironing, shopping, cooking, baking bread, mending clothes, knitting – and of course looking after the children, though the older ones were soon recruited to keep the youngsters out of trouble.

Life for mothers was less arduous in the newer houses, which were so much easier to keep clean, especially with the aid of vacuum cleaners, washing-machines and the other labour-saving devices which were becoming popular in the 1930s. Many middle-class women were expected to give up their jobs, perhaps as teachers or civil servants, when they married, but not so working-class women in the mills and elsewhere. They thus often effectively had two jobs. That they were not simply skivvies in the home is shown by what was a common occurrence in Blackburn and elsewhere on a Friday night. Father came through the door, recalled William Woodruff, a Blackburn-bred man who emigrated to the United States and wrote his two-volume autobiography *The Road to Nab End* and *Beyond Nab End*, and then 'placed his pay packet on the table in the front room. Quietly, mother picked it up; money matters were left to her.' She even bought her husband's cigarettes, stacking them on the mantelpiece above the kitchen fire. Each day the store was reduced, until she renewed it the next week.

Middle-class women found it much easier to look after their homes, and often they would have a maid, but they were subject to other pressures. In particular, the advertising industry proclaimed the importance of youth and beauty. One had to be slim, well dressed and desirable. A popular song of the day insisted that a woman should:

A 1939 copy
of *Woman,*
a magazine
founded in 1937.
Magazines like
these proclaimed
a new cult of
domesticity,
insisting – in
fashionable
Americanised
English – that
'any girl worth
her salt wants
to be the best
housewife ever –
and then some'.

Keep young and beautiful
It's your duty to be beautiful
Keep young and beautiful – if you want to be loved.

This was no comfort, of course, to those who were not young and beautiful to start with; and one doubts that the average hard-pressed Lancashire housewife took much notice of such sentiments. But their daughters may well have, especially as a spate of new women's magazines gave the same message. *Woman's Own* began in 1932, and *Woman,* inaugurated in 1937, soon had a circulation of over one million.

The average Briton, especially the average young Briton, had a very sweet tooth in the 1930s. The passion for sweets and chocolate was well catered for, and not only on local stalls – as this photograph from Kingston Market in 1936 shows – but from new proprietary brands.

The house was the mother's sphere. The father would go out to work, generally for five and a half or even six days a week – and often it would be exhausting work, especially in heavy industry, for instance down a coalmine. He would be first up in the morning, and regular hours of employment usually meant it was possible to tell where he was and what he was doing every hour of the day. Some men would lend a hand with the heavier washing or knead a large bowl of dough before mother started the baking. But unemployment was an enormous psychological, as well as financial, blow to many men. It was common for an unemployed man to refuse to help at all around the house, even if his wife was still working: to do 'women's work' would somehow cast doubts on his manhood. He would become a 'Mary Ann'.

Most children in places like Blackburn recalled the 1930s as a happy time. Food would be remembered particularly vividly, probably because they had often been hungry, and so would cramped conditions, but only because they later experienced more spacious accommodation. At the time they took conditions for granted. Children were endlessly adaptable, and they generally enjoyed themselves, with friendships and games, and with sport, fun and frivolity. School was somewhere you escaped from, but there were plenty of places to escape to. For a time a child's longings would centre on sweets and chocolate. Many local shops specialised in loose sweets, often sold at a farthing a time (aniseed balls, bull's-eyes, banana glories, gobstoppers, treacle toffee and many more), as well as new choice items, like the Mars Bar (first produced in 1932) and

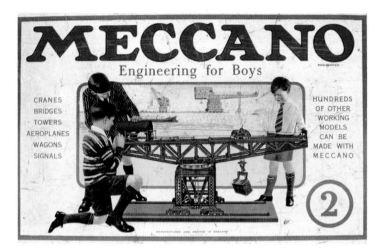

Milky Way (1935). The year 1937 was one to be savoured, with Rolos, Aero and Smarties appearing for the first time. In addition, the 1930s saw new comics, including the *Dandy* and the *Beano*, and toys like Hornby train sets and Meccano, for those who could afford them, and the ubiquitous yo-yo for almost everybody.

Soon, however, a young man's fancy, and a young woman's too, would lightly turn to thoughts of love. Parents would rarely talk to their children about sex, and there was no formal sex education of any kind; but courtship rituals were well established, parents often vacating their front room for hours on end to leave young couples alone – though younger children would often be upstairs with unimpeded views downstairs through ill-fitting floorboards. Weddings were as grand as the parental purses could afford. Often whole families would be kitted out with new clothes, which would sometimes be made to last a lifetime. When William Woodruff's sister got married, there was 'a proper ham and tongue wedding breakfast', followed by trifle and lots to drink. He marvelled that a man 'who resented paying a penny on the tram … could suddenly spend like a profligate', and probably go into debt, for his daughter's wedding. 'Everybody is entitled to go mad once,' his mother decided.

The young couple had a brief honeymoon before settling down in Blackburn, replicating their parents' lives but with aspirations for a better house, a better diet and more consumer goods. Their parents wanted this for them too. Each generation desired something better for their children; and, despite the severity of the Depression in the early 1930s, their wishes were often fulfilled.

Next spread:
The urban landscape was dominated by the factory gates through which a sudden exodus occurred at the end of every shift. Industrial workers were primarily male (other than in cotton factories), with women for the most part looking after the home, family and food.

19

SUN WARMED – SUN LIGHTED
by the radiance of Gas

HOME AND
NEIGHBOURHOOD

S ALFORD BRIDGE was the centre of Blackburn. It was here that the
Roman road had crossed the River Blakewater. Nearby were the
finest buildings and monuments in the town, including St Mary's
Cathedral, built in 1826 to replace a much earlier establishment (and
containing an image of Christ with, according to local people, 'big
workers' hands'), a statue of local worthy Sir Robert Peel and another
of Queen Victoria. Many of the newer buildings had been erected
following Blackburn's 1851 Charter of Incorporation, which had
authorised civil improvements. Corporation Park was laid in 1853,
and the Town Hall was built three years later. The following decade
saw the Cotton Exchange and the Free Library and Museum. The
Market Hall and Clock Tower were constructed in King William
Street, and Thwaites shopping arcade and a new railway station soon
followed, as slum clearance was undertaken.

Blackburn's modernisation had followed a path very familiar in
the north of England and the Midlands. Town centres had become
cleaner, safer and grander, and better administered in Victoria's reign.
Local big-wigs had made substantial donations and town councillors
had bestirred themselves in an effort to make their town the envy of
its neighbours. Nor was entertainment neglected. Blackburn had
three variety theatres by the end of the century, and in 1908 the
Cotton Exchange was made into the town centre's first cinema. In
1922 the Savoy Cinema opened in Bolton Road, and in 1929 it
presented the first 'talkie' to be shown in Blackburn. It boasted a
rarity for this time: a car park. But even this was put in the shade by
the town's first 'super-cinema', the mighty Rialto, which opened in
1931, with a seating capacity of 1,878, plush carpets, a 'Compton'
organ, and a 150-seat restaurant. A similarly grand establishment
opened in 1936, and two years later the Theatre Royal jumped on
the bandwagon and became the Cinema Royal, complete with one of
the best restaurants around. High-profile visitors to Blackburn in the

Opposite:
Most of the new
homes of the
1930s, like the
old ones, were
heated by coal,
but now it was
possible to have
instantaneous and
cleaner heat, with
gas fires.

Right: Blackburn Town Hall in 1899, with the Clock Tower and Market Hall to the right. The legacy of the late-Victorian era dominated the centres of many northern towns in the 1930s.

Below: A view of Blackburn from Corporation Park in 1930, showing the air pollution caused by local mills. During the depression it was possible to count the number of factory chimneys for the first time.

1930s included King George V and Queen Mary, on their Jubilee tour, as well as entertainers Gracie Fields, Charlie Chaplin and Paul Robeson, and Prime Minister Neville Chamberlain.

Not even the 'hungry Thirties' could halt the public's seemingly insatiable demand for entertainment in general and the cinema, and American 'movies', in particular. Towns like Blackburn, and even more so towns with higher unemployment rates, may have lagged behind more prosperous areas in terms of amenities and new developments, but Britain was undoubtedly changing. A ring road was constructed around Blackburn, new factories were built, and at the end of the decade branches of the Co-op, Woolworths and Marks & Spencer opened on Northgate.

To develop city centres was relatively easy, but to improve the housing stock of the majority of the people was anything but. Most of Blackburn's population lived in the houses erected rapidly by local employers – and in this it was similar to dozens of other industrial towns. At the end of the nineteenth century there had been 129 cotton mills in Blackburn, employing around 40 per cent of the local population, and most of them lived in 'two up, two down' houses, huge numbers of which had been built in the smallest possible space (often around forty to the acre), using local stone, slate and clay. Row upon row of these identical cottages were still inhabited in the 1930s.

There were terraces of high-density houses like this in many industrial towns and cities. This photograph is from the dockland area of Newcastle upon Tyne in 1938.

Coal was such a standard fuel in the 1930s that chimney-sweeps were always in demand. There were few female sweeps, but Mrs Charlotte Bursnall was one of them.

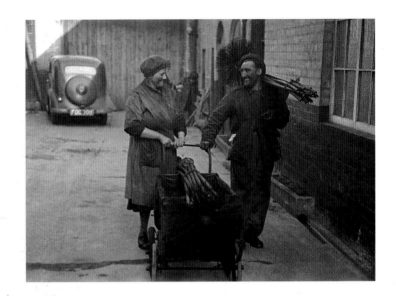

William Woodruff spent part of his childhood in one of these houses, in Griffin Street. There were four whitewashed rooms, each about 9 by 9 feet. The floors were made of flagstones, covered with a scattering of sand which was replaced every week. There was a tiny cobbled yard at the rear. He and his brother shared a bedroom with their parents, while his two sisters slept in the other bedroom. He did

A coalminer in 1939 relaxes after work with a cigarette and prepares to make a pot of tea. Often the only source of heat in houses like this was from the coal range in the kitchen.

not notice the lack of privacy and took for granted his parents' love-making, even before he understood it, as well as the never-ending battle against the bugs that lived in the straw mattresses. The cold and damp, however, were less easy to accept, and the children did not walk to their unheated bedroom but ran. Everything they could find was heaped on top of the beds in winter and sometimes they used layers of newspaper as an extra blanket.

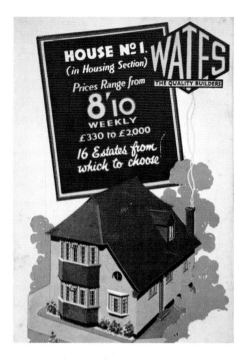

The kitchen, beneath the back bedroom, was the centre of the house, though it was far too small for all six in the household to sit down at once. The coal-burning open range was here, providing heat for the oven, kettles and irons. Here too was the coal store – sometimes delivered while they were eating, in which case a cloud of dust would inevitably settle over their food. The kitchen also contained the house's gas light and gas ring, and the only tap in the house. Woodruff recalled that damp washing often hung from the ceiling for half a week. The front room – called the 'parlour' if people wanted to put on airs – opened directly onto the street, and in winter a heavy curtain would be hung over the door to stop draughts. The front room was used for entertaining and at Christmas, and also for storing precious objects and family photographs. But rarely was the fire lit.

The two bedrooms were supplied with chamber pots, but in the back yard there was a toilet (a 'petty') connected to the main sewer, though without a light or a seat or any means of flushing. 'In summer it stank, in winter you froze to the board.' Next to it was a brick midden, where the family threw their rubbish. In warmer weather this too stank, and attracted clouds of flies.

There were better houses in Blackburn than those in Griffin Street, and indeed for a time the Woodruffs moved to a house in Livingston Road that was at least twice as large. There was a front garden and wrought-iron railings, and William marvelled that the family had a whole room in which to wash. Yet Griffin Street was certainly not unusual, as we can see from George Orwell's descriptions of houses in nearby Wigan, Sheffield and Barnsley. He described 'two up, two down'

The 1930s was a golden age for house-building. This tempting advertisement, offering a house for only 9s 10d a week, was typical of many. However, many purchasers were let down by speculative builders.

Typical semi-detached houses of the 1930s. A motor car, or else proximity to a railway or underground station, was necessary for those increasing numbers who lived in suburbia and commuted to work.

houses with walls falling to pieces, water coming in through the roof and floors that were lopsided. The combined rent and rates for such a house was almost 10 shillings, a substantial portion of most wages in that area, and a high proportion of unemployment benefit. A 'one up, one down', back-to-back house, with rooms measuring 12 by 10 feet, could cost around 7 shillings a week – and there was no back yard and toilet here. Distance to lavatory, noted Orwell curtly, 50 yards. In Wigan alone, there were over two-thousand inhabited houses which had been condemned as unfit.

The Depression was far from an ideal time for expensive housing improvements. And yet improvements there were. They came first in those areas of the country least affected by unemployment and economic crisis. These included huge swathes of the country, especially from 1933 onwards. Interest rates were low and now mortgages could be taken out over twenty-five years rather than the previous sixteen-year period. A massive 2.7 million new houses were built during the 1930s (with an average of around twelve to the acre) and, with the price of imported timber and other materials falling, their cost tumbled. From around £450 for a semi-detached house, twice the annual salary of a professional man, new houses were now within the range of most middle-class families and many working-class families too. The mortgage could be as low as 15 shillings a week, with a £25 deposit.

The typical semi-detached houses of the 1930s were sturdy two-storey constructions, often mock Tudor, with steeply pitched roofs, porches and leaded windows. They contained a front lounge, a dining room and a kitchen, and upstairs a bathroom, two large bedrooms and one small. Outside there would be a small front garden and a larger, secluded back garden, often 30 by 80 feet. Each house would be wired for electricity, so occupiers could use all the latest gadgets. Advertisers insisted that householders' lives would be truly revolutionised.

In the north-west of England the hopes of working-class people for a better home often lay with local councils, and in the 1930s new council houses were being built. In Wigan a new council estate was located at Beech Hill – with row upon row of little red houses, each with a garden, each wired for electricity, and each with a large kitchen and lounge, three bedrooms and a bathroom. They were far more comfortable than the old houses rented from private landlords, and it was far easier to keep warm and clean in them, though Orwell noted that the council insisted on systematically delousing the new tenants.

Late in the decade a housing programme began on green-belt land on the outskirts of Blackburn. Semi-detached houses, each with its own garden, front and back, were built at Livesey, Cherry Tree, Lammack and Pleckgate. Suburbia was to be found even in Blackburn.

A luxurious living room from the 1930s, complete with a stylish suite, classically inspired columns and even a baby grand piano and leopardskin rug. Many home-owners aspired to an interior like this. Perhaps the owners were the original Joneses, with whom everyone had proverbially to keep up.

WORK

MANY PEOPLE in and around Blackburn woke each morning to the sounds of the mill girls' clogs on the cobble streets – if they hadn't already been woken up by the lamplighter or 'knocker-up man': this was the man whose job was to ignite the streets' gas lamps, but he used his pole also to tap on people's bedroom windows until the cry 'We're up!' could be clearly heard. Then the long working day would begin, often ten hours at the start of the 1930s but more usually eight by the end of the decade, plus Saturday mornings.

There were around 130 cotton mills functioning in Blackburn before the 1930s, and at the height of the Depression, in late 1932, as many as one hundred were closed. As it turned out, things improved during and after 1933, and only twenty-nine closed permanently. Cotton was no longer king and Blackburn was no longer the greatest weaving town in the world. At one time the Indian market had absorbed millions of Lancashire loincloths or *dhotis*, but now import duties made them uncompetitive, and local nationalists boycotted them anyway. There was also competition from new synthetic fibres. Rayon, the world's first synthetic fibre, had been developed in Britain and was everywhere by the 1930s; it was joined at the end of the decade by nylon. But there were still jobs at the mills in Blackburn.

People were needed for 'slubbing' – breaking up the bales of cotton, and then cleaning, blending, whirling and pounding them until a sheet of matted tufts (the 'lap') emerged. The lap was then fed between the rollers of a carder to separate the individual fibres. Next the slivers of cotton were drawn across rollers and twisted into threads which were wound onto large spinning bobbins. Spinners would then blend, draw and twist the threads into yarn of various types and thickness. Finally the weavers took over, 'kissing the shuttle', that is drawing the weft of the yarn by sucking it through a small hole at one end of a loom's shuttle. Thus was cloth produced.

Opposite:
Unable to stand upright, and wading through water, a coalminer in 1930 hacks away at the coalface with a pick. George Orwell estimated that such a man probably cut well over 1,000 tons of coal a year.

Lamplighters were frequently seen on Britain's streets in the 1930s, as here at Finsbury Park, London. Sometimes they operated as unofficial alarm clocks for workers who had to be up early.

It was skilful work, and the men and women employed in the mills took it seriously, debating in the evenings how to solve the problems that arose when a new weave or pattern was introduced. It was also hard work involving increasingly complex machinery. As the decade wore on, fewer people were needed; and it was found, for instance, that a deft woman could look after four looms at the same time; but she would be exhausted by the end of her shift. It was also very noisy work. People generally had to shout to make themselves heard, and in time most workers became partially deaf. A characteristic gesture in Blackburn, even outside the mills, was the hand cupped over the ear while a plaintive 'Eh?' was uttered. There were other causes for complaint too. In some mills, anyone arriving even a minute late for work would be docked a disproportionate amount of money, and apprentices would be taken on for seven years but given very little real training and simply allowed to learn the work from assisting more experienced operatives. Soon they would be doing a full day's work, but once the 'apprenticeship' was over and they could claim a full wage, they would often be sacked.

Middle-aged men thrown out of work found it very difficult to get another job, and the longer they were out of work, the scruffier they became and the less attractive they seemed to employers. But boys who had just left school could generally find some sort of work, if only as errand boys, or bookies' runners or assisting in pawnbrokers or other shops – all low-paid jobs. For women too it was sometimes easier. Ever since the Great War had boosted earnings in the factories,

REDMAYNE & ISHERWOOD L^{TD}

BLACKBURN & KIRKHAM

A depiction of one of Blackburn's many mills in the 1930s. Not all of them survived the Depression of the early 1930s, as work was cut back to match falling world demand for cotton goods.

WELDON'S
HOME DRESSMAKER No 500

DAY FROCKS

4³

FREE these 3 Patterns inside

Special
Half-Price
PATTERN
Offer
SEE PAGE 14

As this advertisement from 1935 shows, women's clothing was big business. Yet traditional fabrics like cotton and wool were losing market share to artificial fabrics like rayon, with important consequences for the mill towns of the north of England.

the middle classes had found it difficult to recruit maids and housekeepers. But now the supply became plentiful again. Work could not be turned down, and some employers treated their servants well.

From Blackburn it was possible to see nearby slag-heaps of coal, a visible reminder that the other main occupation in this area was mining. Coal had been a vital commodity in the previous century, when there had been millions of coalminers. It was still necessary for the domestic economy, but now export markets had been lost and coal was being mined much more efficiently outside Britain, for instance in the well-equipped mines of the Ruhr in Germany.

Mining was even harder work than spinning or weaving, and appreciably more dirty and dangerous. Most shifts lasted for seven and a half hours, but they only began once a miner had reached the actual coalface, which might be 100 yards or even a mile from the pit shaft, reached along low tunnels through which it was impossible to walk upright. At the coalseam, some would hack away at the coalface with picks or, in the more modern mines, operate noisy cutting machinery, while 'fillers' shovelled the coal, often at a rate of 2 tons an hour, onto a conveyor belt, in an atmosphere thick with black dust. George Orwell went down several pits in February 1936 and found the journey to and from the coalface exhausting. He wrote that a coalmine fitted his mental image of hell: 'heat, noise, confusion, darkness, foul air, and, above all, unbearably cramped space'.

Orwell also pointed to accidents down the mines. Every year one in six miners was injured, and one in nine hundred was killed, figures that took no account of respiratory diseases like pneumoconiosis. Rockfalls and other hazards like gas explosions were so much taken for granted that each mining company used a rubber stamp (bearing the words 'death stoppage') to denote deductions from pay as compensation for the bereaved. Orwell was also shocked that each week miners had to pay to hire the safety lamp that made their work underground possible, and also that for

Workers prepare a Baby Morris for the London Motor Show at Olympia. The motor industry employed around 400,000 people by the end of the 1930s, but it was not as labour-intensive as the old staple industries.

this arduous, dirty and important work, gross earnings averaged no more than £2 15s a week. He also noted that there were few pit-head baths or showers. Getting clean was therefore awkward at best, impossible at worst. At home a zinc bath-tub would be carried into the kitchen from the back yard, and laboriously filled with kettles or saucepans of boiling water.

Ground crew prepare an aircraft at Croydon Airport in 1931. More and more jobs were created in the aircraft industry as the 1930s progressed, especially once rearmament got under way.

35

Coal and cotton were vital but declining industries in Britain. New employment opportunities were needed, and they were created in the 1930s. Most 'new industries' were located in the south and the Midlands, but as the decade wore on the north too saw the creation of new jobs, especially under the stimulus of rearmament. In 1937 a factory opened at the former Garden Street Mill in Blackburn, with a capacity to manufacture half a million gas masks a week. In the same year a fuse factory opened at Black-a-Moor and an electrical components plant at nearby Little Harwood. Even in Jarrow, by the end of the decade, Imperial Chemical Industries had set up a factory.

Progress was halting in the north, but not so in many areas further south. Here employment mushroomed and flourished. In 1937 there were over two million more people in paid employment in Britain than in 1928. There was remarkable expansion in the aircraft industry, at Bristol and Coventry, and in the building trade (which took on around a third more workers in the first half of the decade) and also in the production of cars at Longbridge in Birmingham, Cowley in Oxford and Dagenham in Essex. By the end of the decade forty-thousand people were employed in the motor industry. The introduction of the assembly line may have lessened job satisfaction, but it lowered the cost of cars, and this in turn stimulated further demand, employment and production. And not only cars were being turned out, but motorcycles, bicycles,

Men constructing the Big Dipper at Blackpool amusement park in 1934. Between 1930 and 1937 around 130,000 new jobs were created in entertainment, sport, hotels and restaurants.

The Hoover Building in west London was designed by Wallis Gilbert & Partners in Art Deco style as the offices for the company's main factory for the production of vacuum cleaners. It opened in 1932, and with the neighbouring Gillette factory and Firestone building, it showed that factories could be imposing structures rather than utilitarian eyesores.

radios, vacuum cleaners, refrigerators, gramophones, toasters, kettles, carpets, furniture and many other items. What had once been considered luxuries had become necessities to many people, especially to those who bought the decade's new houses or who were affected by numerous slick advertising campaigns. The workers needed to produce the new goods in turn became consumers who stimulated still further employment. There seemed no end to the upward spiral. Economic growth led to better roads, new branches of banks and insurance offices, an expansion of retailing, advertising and entertainment, and the prospect of better education and social services.

Work in the new light-engineering factories was cleaner and easier and better paid that in the old staple industries, while the factories themselves – like those established by Hoover, Gillette and Firestone Tyres – did not look like factories at all. With their sleek lines and their gleaming surfaces, they seemed bold examples of what their designers called 'modernity'. It was a brave new world of good wages, high consumption, cleanliness, leisure and hope.

There were two problems, however. Would newsreel images of impoverishment among the unemployed – and there were two million of them at the start of 1939 – spoil enjoyment of the rising tide of affluence? Possibly not. But economic growth also depended on the continuance of the post-war era of peace, and now Britain was in an ominous new pre-war period.

FOOD AND DRINK

WHAT IS A HUMAN BEING? Philosophers have debated the question endlessly. George Orwell, however, had an immediate answer: 'A human being is primarily a bag for putting food into.' Human beings do not only eat and drink, of course, but other functions are secondary in the sense that they cannot take place without nutrition. Many people in Blackburn and elsewhere during the 1930s would have agreed with Orwell, and when food was plentiful, they consumed it with relish.

When times were good the Woodruffs in Blackburn did not merely eat, they gorged. William recalled that Sunday breakfast was a treat, with eggs, bacon, sausages, tomatoes, sweetbreads 'and anything else that could be heaped into the frying pan and onto a plate'. This would be followed by a dinner of roast beef, or a leg of lamb, with vegetables, and then 'a pudding, fruit and balm cakes, dripping with treacle'. (They were not fussy about food that dripped, for there was no tablecloth, only a newspaper.) On Pancake Day or hot cross bun Good Friday, 'we children did nothing but eat'. No one was accused of gluttony, and no one, even his sisters, bothered about their waistlines. They all 'champed and chewed' with relish. The smacking of lips, and even belching and sucking one's fingers, were all ignored, as was slurping tea out of a saucer. 'To eat and drink one's fill was to be blessed.' No one went on a diet and no one was faddish about food. Newspaper photos of the emaciated Indian nationalist leader Mahatma Gandhi were held up as a dire warning of the monumental folly of vegetarianism.

Of course times were not always good, and normally spending on food was limited. Breakfast for working-class families in Blackburn generally consisted of porridge, made with water and served with a little salt. Nothing gave your stomach a lining, and staved off hunger pangs, like porridge. Tea was the normal drink, served piping hot and without milk. Fresh milk was considered a luxury, and anyway it might

Opposite:
Many people in the 1930s ate fresh vegetables, especially if they grew their own, but the modern housewife was under pressure from seductive advertisements to buy processed foods, either in tins or packets.

not be pure and certainly would not keep for long: better to consume condensed milk, if you really had to have milk at all. A midday meal was generally eaten at work by the adults, and might be Lancashire hotpot or something else that could be prepared the night before and heated up or eaten cold. Supper in the evening might consist largely of fish, which was cheap – say 6d a week for one person, if bought just before it 'went off'. Eggs were also in reasonable supply, since many people kept poultry, as were vegetables from local gardens or allotments. No food was ever left on anyone's plate; that would have seemed sinful. Instead they wiped their plates with a handful of bread. They didn't need a dog to eat the scraps: 'We ate them, even if they'd been dropped on the floor.'

Other Lancashire speciality foods, besides hotpot, included meat pies and black puddings, though it was said the best of these all came from a single small shop in Bury, where they had been made for generations. There were also many types of local beer. Fish and chip

Above: Almost everyone seemed to smoke in the 1930s, women as well as men. Woodbines were among the most popular brands. They are presented here as being as traditional and British as the countryside. William Woodruff's father smoked Woodbines, though he called them 'coffin nails'.

Above: It seems that both teachers and doctors recognised the superiority of Typhoo tea over rival brands in the 1930s. George Orwell judged that tea had become 'the Englishman's opium'.

Fish and chips were a regular part of the working-class diet in the 1930s. There were at least 30,000 shops specialising in them at the start of the decade.

shops were also plentiful throughout the region – the region where the combination had originated, in Oldham – with fish generally at 3d and chips at 1d. These would cost more of course if eaten in a café, and these were growing more plentiful in city centres. The apogee of luxury was Harry Ramsden's fish and chip 'palace' in Guiseley near Leeds where customers experienced wall-to-wall carpets, music, leaded windows, and oak panelling and chandeliers modelled on those of London's Ritz Hotel.

Very little fresh fruit was consumed, some even maintaining that it was unhealthy for children. Plums and apples were cheap throughout the 1930s, and yet many mothers only served them stewed. Nor were bananas popular in industrial districts. It was said they were fit only for poor people, not that the poorest indulged in them. Some people only ever ate an orange at Christmas, though ten could sometimes be bought for 5d. J. B. Priestley decided that many working-class people in the north had a rotten diet, adding 'Pity they have not more sense about this.' (He himself found the fare at country pubs quite acceptable. A good lunch – with soup, followed by roast chicken, sausage and two veg, and then a fruit pudding and cheese and biscuits – set him back 2s 6d.)

The food choices of the unemployed were inevitably limited, since a family of four might only have 16 shillings a week to spend on food and fuel. Was it possible to eat properly on such an income? Social

Biscuits, generally broken, had traditionally been weighed and bought at local shops, but now – with the retailing revolution of the 1930s – they were available in packs like this from the new chain stores.

Opposite bottom: A local manager poses outside a Co-operative store, showing an array of tinned goods. The Co-op was a powerful institution between the wars, though its branches, unlike local independent stores, refused to give credit to customers.

reformer Seebohm Rowntree certainly did not think so, and his minute survey of York in 1936 revealed that three-quarters of the unemployed men and their families lived in poverty. Nevertheless a pundit in the *News of the World* claimed that benefits were quite sufficient: an adult could maintain perfect health on a diet consisting largely of wholemeal loaves, margarine, carrots, onions, oranges, cheese and dates for less than 4 shillings. Yet instead, the most common diet among the unemployed in Lancashire and elsewhere comprised white bread and margarine, corned beef, sugar, tea and potatoes. George Orwell decided this was an appalling diet, though adding perceptively that while a millionaire could enjoy breakfasting on Ryvitas and orange juice, someone who was unemployed – that is to say harassed, bored and miserable – did not want dull wholesome food but something a little bit 'tasty'. Unemployment, he decided, was 'an endless misery that has got to be constantly palliated, and especially with tea'.

A growing proportion of the population in the 1930s, however, could afford to eat wisely and well. Almost everyone drank tea, but an increasing number could afford new proprietary brands. 'Everybody Drinks Typhoo', according to a popular advertisement, but there were plenty of alternative brands available, such as Liptons, Lyons, Twinings, Brooke Bond and Ridgeways. Nescafé produced instant coffee from 1932, Bovril boasted that it was the antidote to tiredness, and rather improbably implied that history's great men from Caesar onwards had benefited from its miraculous properties, while Horlicks reputedly prevented 'Night Starvation'. Guinness was simply 'Good For You', a slogan rivalled later in the decade by 'My Goodness, My Guinness'.

Local goods were being replaced in many homes by new national, or international, brands. Kellogg's breakfast cereals became indispensable on many a kitchen table, so much so that the firm decided to open a factory in Manchester in 1938. The sales of new brands of jellies from Rowntree and Chivers, custard powder by Bird's and various spreads such as Marmite and Vitamite also took off. Tinned foods from Heinz and Crosse & Blackwell were also increasingly popular – with their tinned peas, beans, ham, pilchards and assorted tinned fruit. Of course there were the Jeremiahs who detested such convenient and time-saving foods. Orwell, for one, opined that in the long run tinned food might be 'a deadlier weapon than the machine gun', while another pundit thought it was a cause of physical degeneracy. But most people took no notice. Nor did most care that the average Briton was consuming far more sugar that was healthy. The chocolate bars and sweets made by Rowntree, Cadbury and Bassett's sold in ever-increasing numbers, and not only to children.

Food prices were falling, especially for imported items, and so people could afford more. Fresh milk was indeed fresh, and at only 3d a pint it was good value; so were eggs at a shilling a dozen. Diets were becoming more varied and much healthier, complementing a new scientific awareness of food values. National statistics showed that while the consumption of bread fell and that of potatoes remained stable, the consumption of meat, fish, fruit, vegetables, milk and eggs all rose. Yet consumption among the lowest income group was poorest by a long way. Only in the consumption of bread and potatoes did they come close to the national average. An expert computed that the diets of the poorest 4.4 million people in Britain were deficient in protein, fats, carbohydrates, vitamins and minerals, while those of the next group, comprising nine million people, were deficient in all vitamins and minerals.

Items like these – cornflour, yeast extract (Marmite) and beef extract (Bovril) – became standard items in the British food cupboard in the 1930s. Scientists found new, health-giving properties in such foods, for instance in overcoming anaemia.

''Unger's t'best sauce,' William Woodruff's father used to say in Blackburn. It is doubtful whether the better-fed people in the more affluent areas of Britain ever ate with quite the uninhibited relish of those in the industrial areas who had experienced spells of poverty. Even so, their nutrition was likely to promote a healthier and a longer life. As for the unemployed, they lost out, as they did so often in the 1930s. Indeed their nutritional standards were a national scandal. Julian Huxley, in charge of London Zoo, insisted at the end of the decade that if he fed his animals on food of the same quality as that consumed by the unemployed, he would be prosecuted by the RSPCA.

The New and improved
JULYSIA
TONIC HAIRDRESSING
Large size in the NEW wide-neck jar

1/- & 2/-

Shopping and Style

IT IS TEMPTING to imagine that the characteristic style of the 1930s was a drab uniformity. We think of the terraces at football matches filled with men all soberly but scruffily dressed, in dark worn-out suits and flat caps. We think of mill girls walking to work in clogs, with shawls round their heads and shoulders. We may even recall images of the seaside, again with people wearing the same heavy, dark shapeless clothing. Can the temperature at Blackpool or Morecambe really have been so low? Can the 1930s really have been so threadbare?

Finery was not on the agenda for many people, especially during the worst period of the Depression. The unemployed wore clothes until they wore out beyond patching. When a family's children were shod in ill-fitting shoes donated by charities, which soon needed extra cardboard in the soles, it was only to be expected that adults' clothing would be dingy and dismal. People would wear the same things at work as at home; and if they possessed a best set of clothes, this might have to go to the pawnbrokers, along with the best bedding, to tide the family over a particularly bad patch. When it was a choice between new clothes, food or coal, it was not particularly hard to see where priorities had to lie.

Yet we must not stereotype the decade. Most people were in work throughout the 1930s, and if wages declined as the years went on, the prices of goods fell more steeply. People therefore began to feel wealthier. The result of this deflation was greater disposable income, a new wealth that people wanted to spend – for what was the point of saving when prices were temptingly low? By 1935 even the Woodruffs were better off and had, reported William, 'money to spare'.

The threadbare 1930s were also the fashionable 1930s. In time a stigma began to be attached to the wearing of clogs and shawls in the north of England, and most working people acquired a separate set of clothes to wear for their leisure activities. This was certainly true of the younger generation. In Blackburn youths always managed to look

Opposite:
Men did not buy cosmetics in the 1930s; that would have seemed unmanly. But proper care of one's hair was portrayed as a very masculine activity. Julysia, advertised here, and also Brylcreem, were popular.

Right: Popular images of the 1930s derive from photographs like this one, showing a football crowd at The Den, Millwall's home ground, in 1934. Many hard-working men preferred to spend their money on leisure rather than new clothes.

Below: Clothes cost less in the 1930s, and most women could aspire to look chic. For those who could not afford to buy outfits outright, there were often 'payment plans'.

DRESSING GOWNS, BLOUSES AND EVENING COATS MADE IN EXCLUSIVE LIBERTY FABRICS

smarter than their parents, but at Saturday night dances there was an absolute transformation. The boys would have tight-fitting suits, recalled William Woodruff, and the girls would be 'prettied up with their curled hair and white dresses', and also with necklaces, bangles and earrings – admittedly, they were all made of glass, but they still sparkled.

Many people were taking a pride in their appearance, and it was said that Hollywood 'movies' were influencing the way they tried to look (as well as the way they walked and talked and smoked). Many women wanted to be glamorous – to look like Gloria Swanson or Jean Harlow or perhaps Greta Garbo – and the way to do this was to buy a 'film star frock' and to apply lipstick, face powder, rouge and eyebrow pencil. The frock might be daring and reveal amounts of flesh that to the older generation bordered on the scandalous, but no longer was 'a glimpse of stocking' looked upon as something shocking. In the words of the Cole Porter song of 1934, 'Anything goes'. It was said, not always quite accurately, that all women could look like film stars.

In the old days only whores or royalty wore cosmetics, but now ordinary women could be observed opening their handbags for compact and mirror and ostentatiously applying make-up. Also, dresses were now much cheaper and more fashionable. Lighter fabrics like rayon were preferred to cotton or wool. They might not last as long, but then fashions were always changing, so it did not matter. Also colours were brighter, and new zip-fasteners and press-studs gave designers greater freedom to vary styles. Footwear became less utilitarian, with even platform soles and wedge heels for women.

New clothes were expensive, but they could always be bought 'on tick': weekly payments meant the items would cost more overall, but at least that way they were affordable. Anyway, ubiquitous and seductive advertisements made new clothes practically irresistible.

In 1933, passing through Boston in Lincolnshire on his tour of England,

An advertisement from the 1930s for girdle and suspenders. Women were under pressure to conform to an image: they should be shapely but not too shapely.

J. B. Priestley noticed two young women who had obviously modelled themselves on 'certain film stars'. Twenty years ago, he mused, girls like this would have looked different from those in the nearest large towns; they would have had a small-town or even rustic air. 'Now they are almost indistinguishable from girls in a dozen different capitals, for they all have the same models, from Hollywood'. Priestley was exaggerating, out of disgust at what he saw as the Americanisation of British society, but as the 1930s progressed, and more people had more money to spend, Britons certainly began to look smarter. Cheap ready-made clothes meant that, for perhaps the first time, it was not possible immediately to tell someone's class from their dress. No longer did women have to look middle-aged at 30, or old at 40; and men too, despite their reluctance to admit it, might well strive to look like Clark Gable and take care with their appearance.

The hairdryer was one of a growing collection of electrical goods that seemed indispensable to women in the 1930s. Competition between manufacturers helped to keep down the price.

Are you safeguarding the
health of your family with

FRIGIDAIRE ?

*It is an essential to
modern housekeeping !*

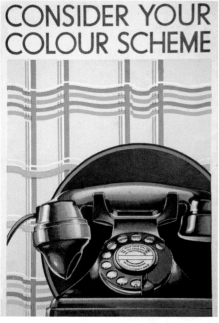

CONSIDER YOUR COLOUR SCHEME

Of course the extra money in people's pockets did not all go on clothes, far from it. George Orwell judged in 1936 that the development of 'cheap luxuries' had helped avert a revolution in Britain. One such luxury was the production of 'cheap smart clothes' but there were others too. Modern electrical science, he noted, was 'showering miracles upon people'; and of course the higher one's income the greater the number of such goods one could afford – though again 'hire purchase' came to the aid of those less well off. By the end of the decade over three-quarters of all new electrical goods were being bought on HP. (It wasn't always such a blessing though, since items did not belong to the purchaser until the final payment had been made: in other words, missing a single payment – even the last – could result in goods being repossessed without a court order.)

Everyone wanted a radio, and almost everyone had one. The price of the cheapest models fell by about a quarter in the 1930s, while sales quadrupled. By 1939 there were almost 9 million licence holders (paying 10 shillings a year to the BBC). Those who bought a new house or whose older house was wired for electricity – and that meant two-thirds of British homes by 1939 – would now want an electric oven, an electric kettle, an electric iron and an electric toaster. And why not a gramophone,

Top: Not everyone could afford a refrigerator in the 1930s, but advertisements like this made women think they ought to have one. Electrical appliances would help middle-class women overcome the appalling servant shortage.

Bottom: Telephones could now be colour-co-ordinated with the décor of one's home. And why not buy a second for the bedroom? Another advertisement asked, 'Why get out of bed to answer the phone?'

a refrigerator and a telephone? Advertisers insisted that such items were not luxuries but necessities. Of course the busy housewife would find life so much easier with a washing-machine, and a vacuum cleaner was another boon. More and more goods seemed to come within people's range, as each year their prices fell; and as the market grew, economies of scale meant they could fall still further. Each year there were new status symbols of suburban life to be purchased, as shown at what became a national institution in the 1930s, the annual Ideal Home Exhibition at Olympia. Nor were cars simply for the few; and there were garden tools to be bought, and plants too ...

DAILY MAIL IDEAL HOME EXHIBITION CATALOGUE OLYMPIA FEB 28-MAR 24

Every year the Ideal Home Exhibition at Olympia kept families up to date with the latest furnishings, fittings and gadgets. Excursions to the exhibition were available from virtually every railway station in the country, and in 1938 600,000 visitors attended.

Shopping was becoming a national hobby, and for some an obsession, especially as shopping became a more pleasant experience. Most shops were still run by small-scale retailers, and there were tens of thousands of small grocers, butchers and bakers, as well as furniture and electrical retailers, and also street-traders, but the decade also saw the growth of what were then called 'combines' or 'multiples' – in other words, chain stores. Here prices were generally lower, the choice of goods was undoubtedly greater and, just as important, all the goods were temptingly on display. Moreover, with well-trained staff often in smart uniforms and refreshments sometimes available in store cafés, shoppers could feel that purchasing goods was a modern and innovative experience. Some stores would deliver bulky goods, those which specialised in hire purchase doing so in unmarked vans, so that the neighbours would think items had been bought outright.

Woolworths, Marks & Spencer, Sainsbury's, the Co-op stores, Selfridges and Boots had all been founded before 1930, but they underwent marked expansion in the decade, the first three even opening new stores on Northgate in Blackburn. Woolworths still stuck to its vaunted policy of selling nothing that cost more than 6d, though only at the exercise of some ingenuity, so that each shoe in a pair would cost this amount and a lid would have to be bought separately from the 6d saucepan. Marks & Spencer built 129 new stores in 1931–5 and extended a further sixty. A café was introduced in its Marble Arch flagship store in 1931, and in the same year they began selling food as well as their own branded clothing. In the decade as a whole their turnover increased tenfold, and they were able to set up their own scientific laboratory to develop and test new fabrics.

Britain was still a very unequal society, but there was undoubted material progress in the 1930s. Even the unemployed benefited from the falling prices that marked the decade, especially after the 10 per cent cut in the dole was made good in 1934. No one had yet coined the phrase, but most Britons had 'never had it so good'.

WOLF
MOTOR CYCLES
for
1932

The WEARWELL CYCLE Cº Lᵗᵈ WOLVERHAMPTON, England

TRANSPORT

E VERY DAY most people in Blackburn around 1930 used the oldest form of transport known to the human race, and the most environmentally friendly: they walked. Their houses had been built as dormitories for the factories and mills, and so it was generally only a short walk to work. Soon, as unemployment mounted, men walked the streets of the town in search of a new job.

Yet there were other forms of transport, including many that owed much to previous centuries. Horses were still commonly used to pull wagons and deliver goods – coal and milk always, and much else besides – and this smacks of a pre-industrial era. The continued use of canals to ferry goods seems very much eighteenth century, though in fact the Blackburn section of the Leeds-Liverpool canal had opened as late as 1810. It was now used much less than in earlier times, but it was still in use, and along it Blackburn's two boatyards still carried on their construction work. Nevertheless, it was the Victorian era that dominated the scene. The local railway station had been opened in 1846 and its two lines were busier than ever. One ran north to south (from Clitheroe to Manchester), the other west to east (from Blackpool and Preston through as far as York). Even more obvious to local people, as they had been since the 1870s, were the town's familiar olive-green and ivory trams – largely because, as one local put it, 'Them trams meks a thunderin' noise!' In 1930 local trams were fitted with upholstered seats for the first time and clocks were erected at each terminus in an attempt to improve punctuality.

Also Victorian, in a sense, was the prevalence of bicycles. The 'safety bicycle', with its chain operating the rear wheel and sometimes with gears, had been popular since 1885, and after the addition of pneumatic tyres in 1888, there were few design innovations. Production had boomed initially. Yet the development of the internal combustion engine and of aircraft made the industry seem decidedly

Opposite: Motorcycles were increasingly popular in the 1930s, being much cheaper than a car and generally more fun to ride. Helmets were not obligatory, though male riders often wore goggles and gauntlets to make themselves look daring. Women, it was hoped, would find the machine irresistibly sexy.

Right: A line of double-decker buses outside Liverpool Street Station in London in 1938. The triumph of buses over the tram or trolley bus was not fully complete, but it was clear that the future lay with them.

Below: The bicycle gained renewed popularity in the 1930s. A new bicycle could be bought on credit for as little as 1s 6d a week.

low-tech, and several British manufacturers, including Rover, Humber and Dunlop, switched to making more profitable machines. Nevertheless falling prices in the 1930s led to another boom, and for much of the decade there were probably ten times as many bikes as cars on the roads. Good profits were made, and Raleigh of Nottingham was so successful that it expanded overseas in 1939.

The scene in Blackburn was similar to that in many other towns, the legacy of the past being important and obvious. You could see it, feel it and smell it. But, also like other places, Blackburn's transport was changing. Trams were finding it hard to compete with the new buses, which could change their routes so much more easily and cheaply. In 1935 the local council decided to replace one tram route with a bus service, and this was just the first of many. Soon – here as elsewhere, in nearby Manchester for instance – it was obvious that trams could no longer compete effectively, and more and more people were carried by buses.

Trains were still important, and they were becoming faster and more luxurious due to rivalry between Britain's four railways companies (London, Midland & Scottish; the Great Western Railway; London & North Eastern Railway; and Southern Railway). On 30 November 1934 the *Flying Scotsman* reached 100 mph, with an average speed of 80 mph over 250 miles, a record that was beaten even before, in July 1938, *Mallard* clocked up a world record for a steam locomotive: 126 mph. The first-class compartments on board these trains were indeed lavish, with proper beds, men's and women's hairdressing salons, and lavatories equipped with dressing tables and full-length mirrors. On board the *Flying Scotsman* corridors were arranged so that window seats would have a view of the magnificent coastal scenery between Newcastle upon Tyne and Edinburgh. Of course amenities for third-class passengers were far more rudimentary, but even they would benefit from the extra speed, and they had only to stand in the corridors to admire the view.

Britons were told in the 1930s that they had the best railway service in the world, and it may even have been true. Particularly noteworthy was Southern Railway's electrification of main lines in the decade, and its extension of London suburban routes. In addition, the Piccadilly, District and Central lines of the London underground were lengthened. Passenger numbers were certainly holding up well. Yet in fact competition from road haulage firms meant that the railways were finding life tough. Prescient observers judged that the future lay with the roads.

In 1935 the London and North Eastern Railway inaugurated the Silver Jubliee service between London and Edinburgh. The last word in speed, comfort and modernity, it set the pace for a battle with its rival, the London, Midland and Scottish railway, that would be cut short only by the war.

To many, mechanisation and speed seemed the keynote of the 1930s. Certainly many drivers ignored speed limits. But most people still walked, and in the countryside there were twice as many horses as tractors.

In the 1920s the sight of a motor car in working-class districts of Blackburn had been a novelty, and many children later recalled seeing one for the first time. But the First World War had revolutionised motor production, and soon driving would cease to be reserved for rich eccentrics. By the 1930s cars were a familiar sight in Blackburn. By 1939 there were two million private cars in Britain – as well as some 600,000 goods vehicles, buses and coaches – and the average price of a car had halved over the previous decade. There were exclusive models in plenty, but the mass market was dominated by Morris, Austin and Ford. Popular models included

Small economical cars were in vogue in the 1930s. At Cowley in Oxfordshire William Morris produced the Morris Minor, which had sold a million models by 1939, and also the more sporty looking two-seater Morris Eight, shown here.

the Austin Seven, with a top speed of 52 mph and doing over 50 miles to the gallon; it had been launched in 1922 but – despite being dubbed the 'motorised pram' by rivals – it was still a bestseller in 1939. Morris's winners included the Morris Minor, which first appeared in 1928, and Morris Eight from 1934. But the most successful car of all was the Ford Model Y, the smallest Ford ever built and the perfect car for a country beginning to pull out of the Depression, reaching 62 mph, achieving 40 miles to the gallon, and

The expansion of car ownership in the 1930s often led to traffic jams, despite road improvements. This photograph was taken during the August Bank Holiday weekend in Kent.

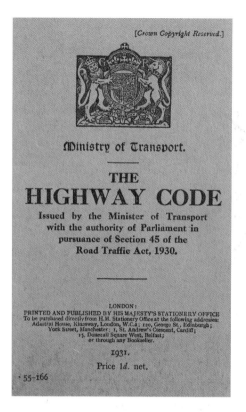

Ministry of Transport.

THE
HIGHWAY CODE

Issued by the Minister of Transport
with the authority of Parliament in
pursuance of Section 45 of the
Road Traffic Act, 1930.

LONDON:

PRINTED AND PUBLISHED BY HIS MAJESTY'S STATIONERY OFFICE
To be purchased directly from H.M. Stationery Office at the following addresses:
Adastral House, Kingsway, London, W.C.2 ; 120, George St., Edinburgh ;
York Street, Manchester ; 1, St. Andrew's Crescent, Cardiff ;
15, Donegall Square West, Belfast ;
or through any Bookseller.

1931.

Price 1d. net.

· 55–166

Britain's first *Highway Code* was published in 1931. It was fairly rudimentary. There were no stopping distances, for instance, and no road signs were explained, but there were large diagrams on hand signals. Few drivers took much notice of it.

costing only £100 new. A massive 39,000 sold in 1933 alone. Almost 160,000 had been bought by 1937, when it was replaced by the Ford Eight, at £120.

Only one in fifteen people owned a car in the late 1930s, but others had motorcycles. The typical motorbike of the 1930s was a 350 or 500cc model, with a single cylinder, twin exhaust pipes and a shiny chromium petrol tank. Technical innovations made it far easier to ride than those of the First World War era. Lamps were powered by a dynamo rather than gas, and engine oil would recirculate automatically, as in a car. The safety record, though, was not good, and too often owners saw riding one as a sport. (William Woodruff used to ride pillion with his sister's boyfriend: they raced across town and thundered down country lanes, whizzing around obstacles at the last moment. The boyfriend even used to show off by riding standing on the seat!) But at least it was possible to fit motorbikes with a sidecar, which made them seem almost an ordinary means of transport.

Britain's road system expanded in the 1930s. While Italy and Germany built prestigious motorways, Britain merely expanded its 'arterial roads'. A ring road was constructed around Blackburn, going from Accrington Road to Bolton Road, in order to alleviate traffic congestion in the town centre, and other main roads in Lancashire were expanded too. J. B. Priestley commented on the new broad and straight road linking Liverpool and Manchester, and that linking Preston to Blackpool, which was festooned with garish advertisements. There were some dual carriageways, but not enough for the growing volume of traffic. The 276-mile Great North Road, for instance, linking London and Newcastle upon Tyne, had no dual carriageway at all.

Priestley also commented on the numbers of 'downright bad drivers' who should not be allowed on the 'crowded and dangerous' roads of 1933. He had a point. In 1930 alone seven thousand people were killed on the roads and another 150,000 injured. Motorists who caused accidents were considered in the courts simply to have made

Britain's first driving test was introduced in 1935, in an effort to reduce what the Minister of Transport called 'mass murder on the roads'. Two hundred examiners were appointed, and many driving instructors appeared – including the racing driver Victoria Worsley, shown here helping her pupil to reverse round a corner.

errors of judgement, so that when a judge sentenced a driver found guilty of manslaughter to three months, he added that this prison sentence was 'no reflection on you morally'. Accidents were just bad luck – especially for the injured.

Some improvements were made. For instance, in 1931 *The Highway Code* was produced and passengers on motorbikes were obliged to sit astride a seat, instead of perching side-saddle on a luggage carrier; and in 1934 the new Minister of Transport, Leslie Hore-Belisha, introduced the famous 'Belisha Beacon' at black-and-white zebra crossings. He also instituted a 30 mph speed limit for built-up areas and, in 1935, devised Britain's first driving test, so that would-be new drivers had to show 'proof of capacity to manipulate a motor car'. Before this all were entitled to drive in Britain, providing they secured a doctor's signature affirming they were physically fit to do so – no matter how incompetent their skill levels or how inconsiderate they might be to pedestrians or fellow motorists. Hore-Belisha admitted that it was an elementary test, but even so around 10 per cent failed it. Probably even more vital for safety was the introduction of cat's-eyes reflectors indicating the centre and edges of the carriageway. Road accidents showed a small fall, but even so over the next few years around 6,500 people were killed each year.

Life in Britain for the foreseeable future would to a large degree be made, and marred, by the irresistible rise of the internal combustion engine.

RECREATION AND ENTERTAINMENT

E LECTRICITY TRANSFORMED a growing proportion of British houses during the 1930s. Wiring the home meant there was less need to escape for warmth or entertainment. There was no television for the vast majority of people, though the first experimental broadcasts began in 1936. Instead families would often listen to the radio together. Light music was popular and so were serialised stories and the news, as well as annual broadcasts like the King's Christmas message, from 1932 onwards, and sports events such as the Grand National and the FA Cup Final. There were also board-games to be played, and many became addicted to the crosswords that were appearing in the newspapers, most famously in *The Times* from January 1930. Some readers complained that space was too precious for such fripperies, and certainly *The Times* did not want to appear to be moving downmarket, so it included a Latin crossword in March. But soon eggheads were vying with each other in boasting of how quickly they could solve every clue.

Newspapers could also be read, of course. William Woodruff's father regularly read the *Blackburn Telegraph* to his wife, who was illiterate. Many people followed national and international news avidly – the latter with increasing trepidation as the decade came to its close. There was also much sensational and titillating news. Crime was declining, and indeed the government was closing down prisons; but there was often some lurid murder to read about, or some sex scandal. Others preferred a good book, especially from libraries or relatively cheap paperbacks available from the middle of the decade. The most popular genre was the murder mystery, and the most popular author was Agatha Christie.

Outside the house, but not far, there was the garden, which constantly demanded attention, or – especially in the north – the allotment. Further afield there was the luxurious picture-palace. The 1930s were the heyday of the cinema. 'Talkies' had arrived in Britain

Opposite:
A trip to the countryside was good, a brisk hike in the fresh air was better, but best of all was actually to stay in the country and truly indulge one's passion for the outdoor life. The Youth Hostels Association made this possible, at only a shilling a night.

The weekly, or twice-weekly, visit to the cinema was a priority for many Britons during the 1930s. In between shows, they could read about their film heroes and heroines in a large number of weekly magazines.

in 1929, and there were even colour films in the 1930s. After the Sunday Entertainment Act of 1932, most cinemas were open seven days a week, and by the end of the decade around 30 million tickets, costing as little as 3d, were being sold every week in Britain's five thousand cinemas. Almost half of Britons went to see a film once a week, while a smaller number would go at least twice. Not even a new house wired for electricity could compete with these luxurious surroundings or with the escapism offered by Hollywood films. The cinemas were especially attractive to young couples. Some even had double seats in the back rows, for the convenience of those who wanted to be especially friendly. The old music halls could not compete, and outside London almost all of them closed, and there were fewer live theatres as the decade progressed too.

Not everyone was content to watch. Amateur dramatics flourished; and J. B. Priestley was surprised, but gratified, to find that above a pub in Newcastle people were rehearsing *The Trojans*. Similarly many tens of thousands took part in sports most weeks, but here too

Working men relax over a beer and a game of dominoes at their local pub, in this photograph from 1938.

the decade was the age of the spectator. Sporting interest in Blackburn was centred on Ewood Park. Blackburn Rovers (a founder member of the Football League in 1888) had won the FA Cup in 1928, the match being broadcast live all over the town, and many supported the team with devotion, being cast into despair when they were relegated to Division Two in 1936, but ecstatic on their promotion in 1939.

County cricket was also popular, and Test matches were followed avidly by many, especially when the 'bodyline' series against Australia hit the headlines in 1932. But it was League cricket that attracted most supporters in Lancashire. Matches would be played on a Saturday afternoon, after work had finished for the week, and some of the world's best

LYCEUM
PANTOMIME
CINDERELLA
TWICE DAILY at 2 and 7
Presented at Popular Prices: **6/6 to 9d.** (plus Tax)
Book of the Words - Price **3d.**

players competed. Nelson employed the West Indian Learie Constantine from 1929 to 1938. Players would have to score quickly or be barracked – but no one ever found it necessary to chivvy the brilliant Constantine. Tennis and golf were also increasingly popular. Neither was a working-class sport, but every Briton knew about Fred Perry's outstanding wins at Wimbledon in 1934, 1935 and 1936, and that Henry Cotton had triumphed at the British Open in 1934 and 1937.

Sport was also important for gambling, another major preoccupation of the 1930s. Between 5 and 7 million people did the football pools every week, spending around £30 million a year. Bets on horse racing could only legally be taken at the courses, but there was a small army of (illegal) bookies' runners at street corners waiting to take punters' money. Gambling provided much-needed, though

The popularity of the cinema undoubtedly harmed the theatre during the 1930s. Nevertheless there were many thriving theatres in London and the provinces. Pantomime was a firm favourite.

AUGUST 1937

HALF DAY EXCURSIONS

FROM KING'S CROSS LIVERPOOL ST MARYLEBONE

LONDON & NORTH EASTERN RAILWAY

Above: A shorter working week in the 1930s meant that more people could take day- or half-day trips, either by train, coach or bus. Transport firms were quick to take advantage of this mini-wanderlust.

often delusory, hope of a better life, especially for the low-paid or unemployed; and the pools or the horses proved a perennial topic of conversation for men at their local pub.

Drinking was another form of recreation in the 1930s, much to the dismay of the moralists. 'Drink meant conviviality and friendship,' noted Woodruff, while for some it provided 'oblivion from a bleak existence.' Another pastime was dancing, with venues varying from local village halls to fine ballrooms. The waltz now seemed old-fashioned, compared to quicksteps, foxtrots and tangos, as well as new crazes like the charleston, black-bottom and stomp, and the jitterbug. There was also cycling and rambling. Tens of thousands of Britons joined cycling clubs in the 1930s and by the end of the decade almost 100,000 were members of the Youth Hostels Association, which offered a bed for a shilling a night. For the less adventurous, day-trips were available. In Blackburn coaches would line up in Blackburn Boulevard, waiting to take day-trippers to the Lake District, the Yorkshire Dales or elsewhere. Northern towns were at least easy to get out of, none being far from the countryside. 'London is much more distant from a real wood than Warrington,' noted one traveller.

The countryside was a revelation to many escapees from the grimy towns, though living there was often harsher than in the towns, most

A parade of women sporting different styles of swimming costume, near the open-air bathing pool in Blackpool in 1936. Their mothers dressed very differently.

Blackpool might have been the holiday destination for Lancastrians, but southerners preferred south-coast resorts like Bournemouth. The climate was kinder, manners more genteel, accommodation more spacious – and the prices higher.

houses being without electricity in 1939 and some having no piped water. Woodruff later recalled that as a Lancashire lad 'I knew not only the squalor of a factory town, I also knew the unforgettable beauty of the surrounding fields, moors, hills and rugged fells.' He, and many others, never forgot joyful summer days playing on the banks of the Ribble, careering down icy hillsides on a homemade sled, or flying a linen kite 'in the ever-present wind'.

Yet day-trips were but a foretaste of what was for many the highlight of their whole year: a week's holiday, generally during the annual Wakes Week that would vary for each mill town (allowing the owners to renew or repair machinery and perform annual stocktaking). In 1936 Billy Butlin opened his first holiday camp, in

Holidays abroad were increasingly popular in the 1930s. For those who could afford it, a transatlantic cruise in luxurious surroundings was the ideal pick-me-up.

Previous page: Billy Butlin's holiday camps proved immensely popular with families, after the first of them opened at Skegness in 1936. They each contained a swimming pool, as the sea on the British coast was often too rough

Skegness, and within a few years there were a hundred such camps, able to accommodate half a million people. But the most characteristic holiday destination for Lancastrians was Blackpool.

As the Depression began to bite, William Woodruff noticed newspaper advertisements for cruises to Madeira and elsewhere, and indeed in 1930 a million British people took a holiday abroad. In 1934 Cunard launched the *Queen Mary* and in 1938 the *Queen Elizabeth*, the biggest liner in the world, variously described as a floating luxury hotel or country mansion. These liners also catered for the middle classes, providing they did not object to occupying 'Tourist Third Class' cabins. Yet it is very doubtful if their customers derived as much enjoyment as the average Lancashire family did from Blackpool, especially as, from 1937, they had a week's holiday with pay.

For the Woodruffs, the holiday began at the crack of dawn on Saturday morning when bags were packed with necessities – not extra clothes, for they had none, but with food which was expensive in Blackpool, including syrup, margarine, tea, sugar, eggs and jam. Then, after stops at pubs en route, where the children waited outside, came the ride on the packed excursion train. Everyone was in good humour and of course no one spoke about cotton: anyone daring to do so would have been 'thrown out onto the track, headfirst'. Like most Blackburn families, when they could afford a trip to the seaside, the Woodruffs shared a single room in a guest house. It was crowded but no one dreamed of grumbling. 'There wasn't a sad face among us. Old and young, we'd promised ourselves a treat … and we were not going to be done out of it.'

The air was bracingly clear, the sun sometimes shone, and there were miles of promenade and long sandy beaches. There were huge ballrooms in Blackpool Tower and in the Winter Gardens, where thousands of spinners and weavers danced on good floors to a Wurlitzer or a fine orchestra. There was a Punch and Judy show, donkey rides, boat trips as far as Morecambe, and the famous Big Wheel. The South Shore was one enormous amusement park. Here there were fiddlers, fortune-tellers, street entertainers, singers, hawkers, sellers of peppermint and pineapple rock, as well as an aquarium, a circus, and a huge open-air bathing pool built not for hundreds but for thousands. There was no boredom, only sheer enjoyment. William Woodruff remembered it as 'bliss'.

Blackpool was an unforgettable experience. The only trouble was that it all had to come to an end. As Woodruff put it, 'After Blackpool, Blackburn air hung like lead.'

EDUCATION AND
SOCIAL SERVICES

POLITICIANS in Britain between the wars insisted that education was 'the most fundamental of all the social services'. The school-leaving age was raised to fourteen years in 1918, and governments promised to reduce class sizes and widen the curriculum. Furthermore, scholarships would ensure that no child missed out on educational opportunity just because his or her parents were poor. The future was surely bright with hope – though not in Blackburn in the 1930s.

Education was not highly valued in many British towns, particularly where typical jobs required manual rather than mental dexterity, or where years of unemployment had sapped ambition. Even so, children had to attend school from the age of five. The choice for the Woodruffs, as for so many between the wars, was between denominational schools: the children could go to either St Philip's (run by the Church of England) or St Peter's (a Catholic school). William's mother was religious, though not committed to either the Catholics or the Protestants, while his father had lost his faith in the war. The result was that the children sometimes switched from one school to the other.

In each there were at least fifty children per class, and education was of a rudimentary type. Teachers were concerned above all to keep order, and they routinely used corporal punishment to maintain discipline. A rod on the seat of the pants was painful, but very much the lesser evil to having the palm of one's hand whacked. At St Peter's, Sister Loyola's prowess with the cane was especially feared. Normally she would deliver three strokes on the hand, her beads and cross rattling with the effort exerted; but sometimes she could not resist a full half dozen. The second priority was rote-learning, interspersed with homilies on sin and hellfire. The whole class would chant endlessly what was on the blackboard: 'Twelve – inches – one – foot ... Three – feet – one – yard ... Fourteen – pounds – one – stone ... Two pints – one quart, four quarts – one gallon'. Pupils would learn the multiplication

Opposite:
Most children, in the 1930s as at other times, crept unwillingly to school, and many found school work unrewarding. But the vast majority contrived to have fun anyway, as with these Glamorgan children enjoying a tortoise race in 1939.

Elementary schoolteachers were not subject specialists. Here a Miss Casey in Bradford acts as football coach to her school team, which in fact had a long unbeaten run in 1936.

tables, the Ten Commandments, and even some good poetry off by heart. They would also learn facts about the British Empire, though not the reasons for its formation, it being simply taken for granted that 'we were better than anybody else'. This was not the sort of learning likely to develop any real understanding; and nor did fear of the dunce's cap produce any love of learning. Curiosity was not encouraged.

William Woodruff described school as 'a holding pen until I entered the mills', and as a place of rest before 'tackling the tasks that awaited me in the real world'. There was no homework, no report cards, and he generally arrived at school having spent a couple of hours delivering newspapers. Hence he tended to doze for the first few hours of every day, before being let off, like so many other children, to deliver family meals to the mills around noon. It was the same for his sister Jenny. She often missed school when there were important things to do. For instance, she looked after her baby brother, often carrying him to their mother in the mill to be suckled, and then taking him home and rocking him to sleep. Despite the official school-leaving age, she got a full-time job in the mill when she was thirteen. William also left school aged thirteen, becoming a delivery boy for a grocer.

There seemed little hope that such people would achieve the scholastic success that would improve their lives. And yet Brenda Woodruff, William's other sister, found schoolwork easy and had wonderful facility with numbers, and – without a book in the house and without special coaching – she actually topped the examinations for eleven-year-olds in Lancashire. She was awarded a scholarship to a secondary school in Preston. The uniform, the train fares, even her books and pencils were all included in the scholarship – but not shoes, and so she did not go. There was little debate between her parents: shoes were expensive and Brenda could be doing real work instead of wasting time with book-learning. She therefore entered the mill and became a 'piecer', an assistant to a spinner. (Nationally, about half the places offered to working-class children at secondary

In a school in Nelson, Lancashire, children play a traffic-awareness game. Such activities may well have been as useful as the rote-learning that formed the staple educational diet at so many schools in the 1930s.

school were turned down in the 1930s.) Education didn't matter, William and his siblings were taught: spinning and weaving mattered. 'The mills were our destiny.' Similarly it was the destiny of wealthier children, even if they were unintelligent or actually downright stupid, to stay on in education, at a grammar school or other fee-paying establishment, until they were sixteen or eighteen.

Ironically, it was the Depression, and William's inability to find real work in the mills, that led to a revolution in his own life. He went to London in search of work, enrolled in evening classes while labouring in a foundry and eventually won a scholarship to Oxford and then studied at Harvard. He became a distinguished professor of history in the United States, Australia and elsewhere – a personal success that throws into relief the failure of the state system in Britain for working-class youths in the 1930s.

What of other social services in the 1930s? Once again the politicians insisted that tremendous strides had been made, and some judged that Britain had more generous

THE SCHOOL AND ADVENTURE ANNUAL FOR GIRLS

Get a Copy Here!

Literacy increased in the 1930s, opening up the world of books to children. A popular annual of adventure stories might be followed by more serious reading.

Men queuing for a job in Wigan in 1939. Several were obviously over the age of sixty-five, but there were various reasons why they might not be getting an old-age pension, and numerous reasons why a state pension would not keep its recipient out of poverty.

and more extensive social provision than anywhere else in the world. There was, for instance, periodic medical examination of children at school, and from 1933 children could have a third of a pint of milk a day at school: it would be free for the poorest or cost a subsidised ½d. The basis of the benefits system, however, was national insurance, and over the years more and more workers had come under its provisions, so that by the end of the 1930s almost all those in paid employment and earning up to £250 a year, even fourteen- to sixteen-year olds, were covered and could claim health and other benefits.

Many found that old-age pensions, at 10 shillings a week, were extremely useful. Insured workers and their wives could claim the pension aged 65, though the non-insured would have to wait till they were 70, and then undergo a means test to see that they needed help. Nevertheless 10 shillings was not, in itself, enough to live on. In York in 1936 Rowntree's survey showed that a fifth of those in poverty were old people, and he described many pensioners 'pinching, scraping ... waiting for the end' – and York was richer than many another northern town. Of course people could have saved while they were working – providing they had any surplus income to save.

It was the same with unemployment benefit. Over the years the scope of benefits had been extended. By 1930 a worker could claim relief indefinitely, not just for any set period of time, and there would be small extra sums for dependants. Yet many believed that the levels of benefit were inadequate, especially once the government introduced a 10 per cent cut in 1931. Benefit for a single man had been 17 shillings, described by Walter Greenwood as 'an impossible pittance', but now

– overnight – this had become 15 shillings. In York, Rowntree showed that, due to the level of unemployment benefit after the cut, almost three-quarters of unemployed men and their families lived in poverty.

When the household means test was introduced in 1931, there was a tremendous outpouring of criticism. Now the total income of a family was all that mattered to the benefits-assessors, so youths' benefits or incomes might deny money to their father. The standard formula for denying someone the dole was as follows: 'The Public Assistance Committee has ruled your household's aggregate incomes sufficient for your needs; therefore, your claim for transitional benefit is disallowed.' Families came under strain and often children were encouraged to leave home once they had left school.

Many benefits were technically on offer in the 1930s, but there seemed to be an array of means tests to stop people receiving them. By 1939 there were no fewer than eighteen different means tests in operation for benefits administered by seven different ministries. The whole system was complex at best, chaotic at worst. If an insured worker were unemployed he could claim an allowance for dependants, but if he were off work because of illness he could not – though he would have just as much need. Were full-time women workers covered? Many assumed so, only to find it virtually impossible to claim benefits, so that very few women were to be seen in the dole queues. And if women did establish their right to benefit, it could be denied them if they turned down work as domestic servants. No wonder that many unemployed people were baffled about just what they could claim, or that they turned for help to the few local experts that existed, often officials of the communist-inspired National Unemployed Workers' Union.

The 10 per cent cut was made good in 1934, as Britain recovered from the Depression. Also, the price of goods was falling, so that the dole was worth more in real terms. Britain's social services in the 1930s were far better than the provision, centred on the workhouse, of earlier decades. But if we look forwards instead of backwards, argued Rowntree, we see how far the living standards of so many people, especially those on benefits, 'fall short of any standard which could be regarded as satisfactory'. Nowhere was this more glaring than in health standards.

PICTURE POST No. 2.

"I HAVE DONE ALL ONE MAN CAN DO TO SAVE PEACE"

80 PAGES OCTOBER 8, 1938   HULTON'S NATIONAL WEEKLY   **3**D Vol. 1. No. 2

It was Neville Chamberlain who, as Minister of Health, Chancellor of the Exchequer and Prime Minister, was responsible for many of the welfare provisions of the 1930s – from contributory old-age pensions to holidays with pay, as well as the household means test and the cut in the dole.

HEALTH

DOCTORS, and even more so hospitals, were to be avoided if at all possible. This was the view of many Britons in the 1930s, especially in working-class areas. Better to turn to patent medicines, especially to prevent the perennial scourge of constipation, which was popularly believed responsible for a whole range of ailments from migraine to frigidity. Did you have a 'furred colon'? – then Bile Beans were the answer, while Eno's Salts would make the crucial digestive difference between 'Mr Can and Mr Can't'. Or one could just have cornflakes for breakfast: those who consumed them would 'never miss a day' said the advertisers – ignoring the fact that such processed cereals were low in fibre and therefore in roughage.

There were herbal or folk remedies for a whole range of minor medical problems, and there were generally local people who would advise, or even prepare potions, especially 'wise women'. Of course no one considered them to be witches, not in the enlightened 1930s, but many believed there was something slightly supernatural about them and held their prowess in awe. They would know what to do to speed a cough or cold to its conclusion, and their poultices were generally efficacious in the cure of boils – and what they did not know about constipation simply wasn't knowledge. For extreme cases they would recommend an enema – undoubtedly effective, though not if the original problem was a stomach ulcer or appendicitis. These women might also help with 'female complaints', including unwanted pregnancies, and could double up as unofficial midwives. They were also called in sometimes to 'lay out' the dead.

Visiting a doctor, or going to hospital, was for some a last resort. In Blackburn William Woodruff's father had experienced doctors during the Great War, in which he had been gassed, and had no wish to do so again. Yet when he collapsed at work with severe abdominal pains, the local doctor was called in. Dr Grieves soon bundled the patient into an ambulance bound for the local hospital, but he never arrived.

Opposite:
Patent medicines were very popular in the 1930s. Here Andrews Liver Salts, designed to combat over-indulgence and to have a mild laxative effect, are being eagerly consumed, almost as a night-time treat, by two children.

Fearing that if he ever entered a hospital he would die, Mr Woodruff persuaded the ambulance driver to turn round and take him home. There he resorted to a traditional folk remedy – fistfuls of bread being steamed over a kettle, placed between sheets of brown paper, and applied to the inflamed area – which apparently cured the problem.

The basis of the medical system in Britain dated back to 1911 and the National Insurance system. Those workers who were covered could not only claim unemployment benefit, they were also entitled to free treatment from a general practitioner. Admittedly these 'panel' patients would not be treated as well as fee-paying, private patients: the latter would have longer consultations, could make appointments instead of queuing in a waiting room, and were more likely to get a home visit. It is also true that GPs often gave out placebos that were no better than patent or herbal remedies. They had no antibiotics; penicillin, though discovered in 1928, was not available for use till 1941. In addition, the main killers of the decade, like heart and respiratory diseases and tuberculosis, were due to inadequate nutrition and housing, which doctors had no control over and no cure for. Nevertheless this system undoubtedly made a real difference to millions of workers.

The main problem with health care in the 1930s was that the National Insurance system did not go far enough. It included no dental or optical treatment, and little hospital care; nor did it cover the dependants of insured workers, except at childbirth.

Painkillers like 'Aspro', containing acetylsalicylic acid, or aspirin, were consumed in large quantities by those unwilling to go to a doctor or unable to afford the fees. Only insured workers were treated freely by a general practitioner.

DOES NOT HARM THE HEART

'Teeth is just a misery,' George Orwell was told in Wigan. Toothache was indeed a perennial problem, and dentists were expensive. When the young William Woodruff could bear the awful pain no longer and was taken to a dentist, he had to have the cheapest treatment, extraction at 2 shillings rather than a filling at 3s 6d, although the dentist has wanted to save a 'perfectly good tooth'. Some people decided on pre-emptive action: as a special birthday present, perhaps at the age of 21, they would have all their teeth out, such 'wholesale extraction' being quite a cause for celebration. Of course they could not afford to have made-to-measure dentures, but sets of false teeth would be available at Woolworths or elsewhere. Nor could everyone afford to visit the optician and have special prescription lenses, but again there would be a choice of made-up glasses.

A person simply chose the ones that provided the best vision, or the least bad.

Many municipal hospitals in the 1930s were converted workhouses – in Blackburn the Union Workhouse at Whinney Heights had become the Queen's Park Hospital – and most people dreaded them, with good reason. They tended to be bare, draughty places, with concrete floors that emphasised every footstep. Each ward would contain row upon row of iron beds. It was said that hopeless cases would be put in beds nearest the doors, so that corpses could be removed on a hooded trolley with minimum

fuss. The next day, as Walter Greenwood wrote, the new occupant of such a bed would be treated to 'a running reminiscence, from both sides, of the virtues and manner of death of their predecessor'. But that was perhaps preferable to the other noises Greenwood heard: 'the unearthly moans of a man dying unattended in some remote part of the ward ... the jabberings of another patient recovering from a recently administered anaesthetic.' There were better hospitals of course, but not many that were likely to treat low-paid workers or their families.

Derelict and slum housing in Newcastle. For most people in the 1930s, health depended on decent housing and food, rather than on medical treatment.

Women and children were largely excluded from the state system of health care. The ideal was that their husbands would insure them privately, or else save up enough money for treatment as and when it was needed; but the ideal rarely became reality.

Childbirth was hazardous in the 1930s. In hospitals mothers were increasingly given pain relief during labour, though most babies were born at home in the decade.

Only in emergencies would the uninsured consult a doctor, and GPs then tended to charge them less than the going rate, making good the loss by charging extra to wealthier patients. But many women would simply put up with ailments, some even finding that it was possible to live a more or less normal life for years with, for instance, a prolapsed uterus.

Children at school would at least undergo regular medical inspection, but women could only expect free help when they gave birth – and this was not always of good quality. It was best to avoid a GP if at all possible, especially since a doctor coming straight from a hospital or mortuary, and failing to wash his hands thoroughly, might unwittingly infect a mother. Midwives were generally more competent, though until late in the decade there were too few of them, and often the only help working-class mothers received was from friends and neighbours. Many accepted without quibble that childbirth was a painful and dangerous undertaking. It was, however, becoming widely known that anaesthetic reduced the pain of delivery, and some

A sugar-rich diet and a fear of or inability to pay a dentist meant many Britons' teeth were in a shocking state. Some preferred to have them all out rather than let the teeth decay one by one.

Most GPs were treating patients in the 1930s much as they had done over several decades, but Britain's voluntary hospitals were often equipped with the latest medical technology. Here a woman is being X-rayed at University College Hospital in London.

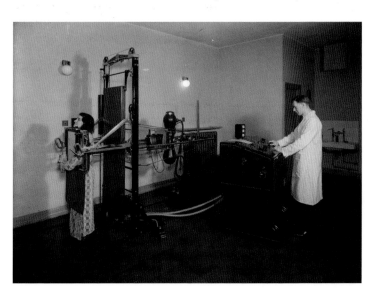

midwives were able to administer relief paid for by charitable donations – first of all, crushable chloroform capsules and later, 'gas and air' (roughly equal measure of nitrous oxide and air, from the Minnitt Gas and Air apparatus). But industrial areas tended to be the last to see such improvements.

Statistics showed that mortality rates for infants who survived birth were falling (from 68 per 1,000 in 1930 to 55 by 1938) and that people were on average living longer. (William Woodruff, who was born in 1916, lived to 92.) Yet maternal mortality rates were strangely resistant to improvement. This was because of disproportionately high rates among the poor, so that maternal mortality rates were over six times as high in Durham as in Middlesex.

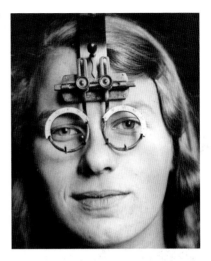

An eye test, to decide the best lenses to correct the sight in each eye, was an elementary procedure, but many Britons never saw an optician in the 1930s and bought their spectacles from chain stores.

A report in 1938 estimated that over three thousand women a year were dying during childbirth in the depressed areas. The main reason for this was that many mothers were in such poor physical condition. Inadequate housing and sanitation were partly responsible, but the root of the problem was nutritional. Many women, the report found, were 'literally starving themselves to death in order to feed and clothe the children reasonably well'.

Health undoubtedly improved in Britain as a whole during the 1930s. The Jeremiahs who insisted that things were getting worse and worse lacked true perspective. In 1936, in Trafalgar Square, George Orwell was struck 'by the physical degeneracy of modern England … puny limbs, sickly faces … hardly a well-built man or a decent-looking woman … Where are the monstrous men with chests like barrels and monstrous moustaches like the wings of eagles who strode across my childhood's gaze twenty or thirty years ago?' But Orwell was quite wrong in supposing that physically Britons had declined since 1914. People as a whole were healthier in the 1930s than in the previous decades. It is true that, after the dole was cut in 1931, medical officers of health from all over the country reported increases in the incidence of rickets among children; true also that doles and diets were inadequate. True, but not the whole truth.

Working-class schoolboys were on average 4 inches shorter than their public-school counterparts in the 1930s. Yet on average schoolboys from areas of poverty and unemployment grew up to be several inches taller than their fathers. This was the sort of progress Britain saw in that paradoxical decade, the 1930s.

PLACES TO VISIT

Nuffield Place, Huntercombe, near Henley, RG9 5RY.

    Website: www.nuffield-place.com

    The home of Lord Nuffield, the founder of Morris Motors, and a fine
example of an upper-class house from the 1930s.

People's History Museum, Manchester, Spinningfields, Manchester M3 3ER.

    Website: www.phm.org.uk

    Contains many exhibits relating to the 1930s, and to the Jarrow
Crusade in particular.

Central Library, Blackburn, Lancashire BB2 1AG.

    Website: www.blackburn.gov.uk

    The Community History section, on the second floor, contains a wealth
of local photographs and newspapers.

Avoncroft Museum of Historic Buildings, Stoke Heath, Bromsgrove,
Worcestershire B60 4JR.

    Website: www.avoncroftorg.uk

    1945 prefab with furnishings that reflect 1930s style.

Bakelite Museum, Orchard Mill, Williton, Taunton, Somerset TA4 4NS.

    A museum of plastic which includes a range of 1930s household
goods.

Design Museum, Shad Thames, London SE1 2YD.

    Website: www.designmuseum.org

    Includes many examples of classics 1930s design.

Geffrye Museum, Kingsland Road, London E2 8EA.

    Website: www.geffrye-museum. org.uk

    A museum of domestic interiors, which includes a suburban lounge of
the mid-1930s.

High Cross House, Dartington, Totnes, Devon

    Website: www.dartingtonhall.org.uk

    One of a collection of fine 1930s Modernist buildings alongside the
medieval house.

Museum of Domestic Design and Architecture, Middlesex University, Cat Hill,
Barnet, Hertfordshire EN4 BHT.

    Website: www.moda.mdx.ac.uk

Victoria and Albert Museum, Cromwell Road, London SW7 2RL.

    Website: www. vam.ac.uk

    National museum of arts and design contains a wide range of fine
examples of 1930s fashion, accoutrements and objects of daily life.

Museum of Brands, Advertising and Packaging, 2 Colville Mews, Lonsdale
Road, Notting Hill, London, W11 2AR.

    Website: www.museumofbrands.com.

    Museum of ephemera and collectables of all kinds, the source of many
of the colour illustrations in this book.

INDEX